Letter at the End of Winter

University of Central Florida
Contemporary Poetry Series

George Bogin, *In a Surf of Strangers*
Van K. Brock, *The Hard Essential Landscape*
Rebecca McClanahan Devet, *Mother Tongue*
Gerald Duff, *Calling Collect*
Malcolm Glass, *Bone Love*
Susan Hartman, *Dumb Show*
Lola Haskins, *Planting the Children*
Roald Hoffmann, *The Metamict State*
Hannah Kahn, *Time, Wait*
Michael McFee, *Plain Air*
Richard Michelson, *Tap Dancing for the Relatives*
David Posner, *The Sandpipers*
Nicholas Rinaldi, *We Have Lost Our Fathers*
CarolAnn Russell, *The Red Envelope*
Robert Siegel, *In a Pig's Eye*
Edmund Skellings, *Face Value*
Edmund Skellings, *Heart Attacks*
Don Stap, *Letter at the End of Winter*

Letter at the End of Winter

poems by

Don Stap

UNIVERSITY PRESSES OF FLORIDA
University of Central Florida Press
Orlando

Printed in the U.S.A. on acid-free paper. ∞

Library of Congress Cataloging in Publication Data
Stap, Don.
  Letter at the end of winter.
  (University of Central Florida contemporary poetry series)

  I. Title. II. Series.
PS3569.T3345L4   1986   811'.54   87-2093
ISBN 0-8130-0859-X (alk. paper)

University Presses of Florida, the agency of the State of
Florida's university system for the publication of scholarly
and creative works, operates under policies adopted by the
Board of Regents. Its offices are located at 15 Northwest
15th Street, Gainesville, Florida 32603.

Acknowledgments

I thank the following periodicals for permission to reprint poems which first appeared in them: *The American Scholar, Celery, The Chariton Review, Florida Review, The Greenfield Review, Green River Review, Grove, The North American Review, The Massachusetts Review, Orca, Passages North, Poetry, Poetry Northwest, Quarterly West, Texas Quarterly,* and *Western Humanities Review.*

In addition, "Trying to Write" originally appeared in *Poetry* and is reprinted with permission.

The epigraph to part 1 is from *All the Strange Hours* by Loren Eiseley, published by Charles Scribner's Sons, 1975. The poem at the beginning of part 2 is titled "Boating on Wu Sung River." It is reprinted from Kenneth Rexroth's *New Poems,* copyright 1974 by Kenneth Rexroth, and is reprinted by permission of New Directions Publishing Corporation. The lines at the beginning of part 3 are from "Snow," from *Selected Poems* by Vladimir Holan, translated by Jarmila and Ian Milner (Penguin Modern European Poets, 1971), copyright 1971 by Vladimir Holan, translation copyright 1971 by Jarmila and Ian Milner, p. 82. They are reproduced by permission of Penguin Books Ltd. The epigraph to "Our Bodies Falling Through the Heavens" is from "Lines Upon Leaving a Sanitarium," copyright *"The Word,"* 1937, by Theodore Roethke from *The Collected Poems of Theodore Roethke,* reprinted with permission of Doubleday & Company, Inc.

I also wish to thank the Michigan Council for the Arts for a Creative Artist Grant for 1982−83.

And I am especially grateful to Robert Mezey and Richard Schramm for their comments and suggestions on the poems and their steady support.

for Kristine

Contents

I

The Kalamazoo River, 3
Fever, 4
The Outskirts, 5
Jacob Stap, 6
Fall Weather, 7
Moving West 8
A Handful of Poems for My Father, 11
  Driving Home
  Home
  Dream of the First Night
  Daydreams
  Returning by Plane
  Another Life
  In the House by the Highway
Things That Look the Same, 18
Remember? 19

II

Fireflies, 23
These Birds, This Life, 24
Full Moon, 25
What Will You Remember? 27
At Night, 28
The Big People, 29
The Arranged Hours, 30
From a Photograph, 31
Seashells, Cape Hatteras, 32
Late December, No Sign of Snow, 33

The Other One, 34
For Inese, 36
Crow, Grandfather, 37

III

Inside a Life, 41
Walking at Midnight, 43
Trying to Write, 44
A Terrible Life, 45
Crooked Lake, 1978, 46
A Small Joy or Sadness, 47
Memorial Day, 48
Tonight, Sitting Down to Write, 49
Afraid to Speak, 50
Giving Birth, 51
Our Bodies Falling Through the Heavens, 53
All Day, 55
Letter at the End of Winter, 57
Walking in My Grandfather's Fields, 58

About the Author, 60

I

"Nothing perishes, it is merely lost. . . .
Nothing is lost, but it can never be again
as it was."
                    — *Loren Eiseley*

The Kalamazoo River

East of Kalamazoo
the old celery fields blacken
as the summer begins
and the river turns sullen and slow.
The days are too long for the mothers.
They are as blank as the abandoned greenhouses
that close their eyes each evening
on the treelined streets of Comstock.

The fathers and grandfathers,
good Christians
sift homeward through the streets
when the shift changes at the paper mill,
the first straw-colored light
emptying into the world.
Out of those caverns blasted with noise
they come to turn a latch
lean into gray rooms
and touch their wives
rolling over for the hundredth time.

And we are the sons and daughters
who've walked too far from home
who live now in the seasons between seasons
where the smallest flowers bloom.
No one remembers that it was the motion of water
that brought them to life
that as children they played by water
and now only the voice of water
passes through their dreams . . .
they are somewhere else
years away and happy with their lives
in the river towns of Kalamazoo
Plainwell, Paw Paw, Saugatuck. . . .

Fever

Behind my childhood house
an owl glides down
toward a noise in the dark furrows.
But the mice have grown as large
as work boots from eating wheat that shimmers
like a rainbow at midnight.
They snatch the owl out of his low sweep
and feast on the moon in his eyes.

The room throbbing,
I dream of the owl
of the chemical fields where luminescent
wheat blows in the wind.
An oak tree, hollow from top
to bottom, large enough
for a skinny boy to fit into
holds all the light lost
from the world each day.

A jar of fireflies sits on the floor
at the foot of my bed.
I can't see it, but I know it's there.
Like a flock of birds turning in flight.
Like the one who enters my room
while I'm asleep and touches
my forehead the way air
above the river touches the water.

The Outskirts

A skunk smuggles himself
through the shadow of boxcars
and along the tracks that mark
the outskirts of town.
He hurries toward the smell
of slow water and sleepless horses.
The moon slides off his back into a cloud.
Headlights, taking sudden aim, spill the odor
of sour earth over James Creek Bridge.

By day locust clack out a song
in the dry weeds, and ten-year-olds,
recording their afternoons by the burrs
and stick-tights on their socks
will scratch until way past supper.
Nothing comes of this time of year
of this place on the edge of town.
The fields, useless after harvest
hold out their legend of summer in braille.

Jacob Stap
1893–1976

Farmer and carpenter
soldier in the Old Country
stubborn old Dutchman alone for thirty years
in the whitewashed house falling in on itself
its walls leaning like a house of cards. . . .

Each winter your dirt cellar was ankle-deep with walnuts.
The well water tasted like the night air in the woods
and there were bad dreams when your big face
swung like a lantern above me.
I closed my eyes tighter, but it was no good.

Now I fear your absence.
Forty-seven acres of your land is planted
with corn this year. Your land, I thought.
A new shopping center lights up a corner of the country sky.

It's all slipping away.
You never knew why,
and I see now that I won't either.
On your deathbed you were climbing a ladder.
My mother was trying to help you down.
Steady girlie, you said,
hold it for me at the bottom.

Fall Weather

At the edge of the park
a few bees are adrift near my shoetops.
I stoop down and find
from a pear tree planted the year before
the perfect fruit, so small
it can be eaten whole.

*

Far back, she's leaning over
a sink of dishes tapping
on the kitchen window.
She wipes the fog from the glass
with the heel of her fist
polishing a little circle
that closes on her before she's finished.
I used to know what she meant:
across the field, at the horizon
a sheet of thin, bloodless light
was standing on ice.
It was time to come in.

*

Every year I wanted so much
the past and present both
and now it's more than I wish for
a familiar light teetering
on the far ridges
and this clarity
once every year
when the lawns are at their widest.

Moving West

1. Interstate 80, Nebraska

It takes a long time to drive through Nebraska
three or four years at least,
if you're paying attention
a millennium or two.
Behind you the highway sneaks back to Iowa.
Ahead it disappears in the Pleistocene
somewhere near Loren Eiseley's backyard.

All day down long hills through
green valleys into
darkness nothing changes
over and over it rolls on inside me.
The eyes of a raccoon flash near the highway fence.
The cow-catchers at the exits that go nowhere
haven't caught a single cow today.
There's too much grass elsewhere
too far to roam.

2. Wyoming: Focusing on Infinity

The camera, focused on infinity
freezes a small herd of antelope the moment they turn to flee.

A year later they will be mere specks on the hillside,
then only a whirl of dust
then loose stones.
We will turn that page in the album quickly.

Later that night, I dream
of joining the long sleep of fish
who entered the shallows here centuries ago
and are just now surfacing in sandstone.

3. Salt Lake City

Like a string of boxcars crossing the salt flats
a wind from Nevada arrives right on time
scattering seagulls all over the city.

Like birds made of paper they are tossed about.
Like scissors their wings cut through the dry air.
Wobbling on sealegs across the immaculate sidewalks
they belong in this desert as much as I do.

Standing on these wide, flat streets
coordinated as if the map came before the land
I can almost feel the earth tilt east,
thin, rainless clouds scaling the Rockies.

4. Things Disappearing in Arizona

I make a list:
boat-tailed grackles
stands of bottlebrush at the roadside
a roadrunner poised in the narrow shade of a telephone pole
the thousand yellow eyes of the creosote bush squinting into
    the sun
and most of all
light running off the desert
like water
into the arroyos.

Three miles out of Grasshopper Junction
there is something beside the road.
An old man crouched in the ditch?
No, only a flapping coat caught on a cactus

9

a waving hand sinking in the rearview mirror.
I've come all this way to see clearly in the new western light
and now I can't be sure.
I look again.

A Handful of Poems for My Father

1. Driving Home

Up at five. On the road by six.
I couldn't tell you which blurs of light
are moving and which are standing still.

The dream I woke with is huddled inside
keeping warm, the car rocking in the wind.

Up ahead a blemish waters the skyline,
blood rising to an old wound.

Four hundred miles away
my mother rolls over in bed
lifts the curtain an inch
and peers out.
Nothing moves and nothing shines.

2. Home

The sky over my father's house
is clear blue,
a strong wind blowing in.

I have forgiven him everything
and myself nothing.
Like father, like son.

Once where the path into the woods begins
I saw him lean over
and look down the long tunnel of trees
to where I was standing
peering back at him.

Unable to see who it was,
he stood motionless for a long time.
Fish in still water hold the same attitude.
And animals staring into the endless beams of light.

3. Dream of the First Night

The room I slept in as a child
is still dark, even in memory.

Adrift on the black water
of a lake somewhere in the north
and sometime after midnight,
one arm hangs over the side of the raft
and my fingers, slightly curled
trail in the water.

They darken, deeper than ebony
and the music of the past begins
tremor, whisper, bubbles breaking around the skin.

4. Daydreams

Ten years gone by
and I still don't know what to keep
and what to throw away.
These boxes in the basement
hold the scraps of a life
I want to remember, the sweet pain of it
as light as the dust that comes off on my hands.

How is it I didn't marry this girl
who wrote me letters on such delicate blue paper
and said nothing I wanted to hear?

Luck, I guess. And her long brown hair
her small sad kisses.

5. Returning by Plane

The earth so far below
looks terribly old, the land barren
shrouded in mists.

We pass over blue water
white rivers of snow
and over brown wrinkled plains no one wants.

We're moving so slowly
if I woke from this dream
I would still be dreaming.

I can hear that far-off sound—
a field of bees
bowing over the clover

and one of them gone mad
tracing and retracing
some vague message in the air
directions I cannot follow.

6. Another Life

Some nights when I come home late
I stand in the driveway looking at the house,
thick yellow light swarming about the windows

and I don't believe any of it.
But there it is, someone's life.

Take it or leave it.

7. In the House by the Highway

Am I to listen all night
to the cars going by
each one another false prayer
half-gathered, then hushed,

and those same watery lights
on the walls, folding up
as they always have?

Above the creaking roof
the moon's keen sickle
reaps a harvest of stars.
There are too many lives
too much distance between them.

And still I lie here
eyes open
one hand growing transparent.

Things That Look the Same

Evening blue. The flame turned low.
The sky fills with a long rambling story
or is it blackbirds gathering for the journey?
Or the thoughts of a man sitting in one room too long?

On this far sandy edge of summer
an entire month caves in,
or is it me giving up again?

Back at the millpond
I stand on the railroad tracks,
two heavy spears blazing with white heat.
One is as infinite as the life I pretend.
The other one—parallel and unforgiving
always so close by—is the way it really is.

Or is it the other way around?
Some things look the same.

Anyway, they go on and on never touching
all the way back to Minnesota,
where every summer a boy spent his pennies on them
against his mother's wishes and threats
and finally the stories of trains derailing
just because some kid was looking to buy luck cheap
with a flattened one-cent piece.

Now, the pond is deepening with shadows
or is it the dark face of my complaints
or something I can't remember until it's too late?
Or is it just the day breathing heavy
after all is said and done?

Remember?

My mother is telling the family stories again.
We are standing behind the house
and I look past her into what's left of my grandfather's fields
after death, taxes, and another night falling fast.

I look far away, past the last treeline
then back. Where she was standing
there are only a few blackbirds in a leafless tree.
Her eyes, I'd swear, were never that dark
her love never so transparent.

"Remember," she was saying, "turkeys
will drown in a rainstorm after a drought—
they'll throw their heads back to drink
and won't know when to stop."
I know what she means.

My eye catches two mourning doves whistling out over the
    field.
One more disappearing act.
The plowed earth swells toward the skyline
where the last pure light lay a moment ago.

Remember?

II

The setting sun leaks through the sparse,
Slender, flowering rushes.
For half a day I've been alone
Chanting poems
And haven't crossed the river.
Only the egrets have understood me.
Time after time they come
Stand on one leg and look in the boat window.

—*Wang Yu Ch'en,*
tr. by Kenneth Rexroth

Fireflies

We knew they were magic
so we stuffed them into a mason jar
and ran home along the tractor path.
Another time, on a bluff above Lake Michigan
we found a rotten log filled
with trails of light.
Glowworms, you said and
the girls at our sides leaned in against us
and I felt a feather drawn
down the length of my body.

Tonight, older by several years
and by this house
and these rooms where the worries are kept,
I watch the yard.
A cloud of gnats, about to take form
crumbles into confusion again.
And yet there are these small lights
in the hedgerow the trees
and then in the open.
I reach out quickly and close
my hand on what has just gone dark
so how do I know for sure?
Moonlight is falling across the lawn
like warm shallow water.
I'm standing in it up to my knees.

These Birds, This Life

All day, the finch
color of spilled wine in the afternoon sun
and a clear hurried song
about to dissolve.

Turn to look and all I'd see
was a branch springing
up and down, the tree
green and empty.
These birds, I'm always saying, *this life*
as if there's another.

Head flung back, looking
into the sun after a hawk
I have gone blind,
seen the outline of wings
seared on the inner darkness
felt the burning die
before it reached my feet.
I could follow everything that is sinking
on swift currents, everything that is dark
and wears a hood of brightness
and tears open the sky.

It is like this.
Or else, on a frozen January day
the marsh reeds in splints of ice
the search given up
I turn around, and five feet away
in perfect silence. . . .

Full Moon

—for Sandra

At 10,000 feet
a woman is skiing cross country
the pinpoint light
of snowflakes spreading through her
and the wine
and the powder of the moon
sparkling beneath the skis.
She turns to take a slope,
pushes off
a white petal sinking in water.

The papers on my desk rise
to the moons in my fingertips.
The hundred-year-old maple floats
outside the window
another growth ring forming
another watermark of the moon.
Kathy calls from the hospital:
two more suicides and
three hours yet until dawn.
The tides in their blood, she says.
The night sails on
the moon slides behind the clouds.
I stay awake waiting
for my friend to come home.

In awhile
a cat crosses the highway
gray as the foothills
his green eyes lit from within.
He has seen the gold-tipped thistles
and transparent grasses
of another country
and heard in the east a story of
a woman coming down the mountain
the first light
slung over her back.

What Will You Remember?

At the hour of sunset
the curled-back fur of the clouds
the great, slow sun descending
the mountains drenched
a last bullet of light,
the pale wine drunk deep.
And those several ridges seen only in this dusky scattering
and the seagulls coasting the foothills
and the wind swinging larger through the yard
and the apricot trees the field of turned-up rocks
the cats wandering home.

The way it settles
answers to blood
turns to go in
presses its hands against the smooth glass of night
and is still—
before the lights tightening all over the city
the minutes the hours
the flashes from the sheet metal shop
the heavy hammers going down in the train yard
all flung back to a man standing at a window.

At Night

At night, on an unfamiliar street
I look into a house where a young woman
is ironing a blouse. She is naked
from the waist up. I stand
in the shadow of a tree and watch her
move the iron over the collar
then the sleeves. She holds up
the blouse to the light coming from
the only lamp and begins to dance,
two-stepping with more and more
exaggeration toward a corner
I cannot see, toward the laughter
drawing her into his arms.

The Big People

The lights go out.
The big people go into their room to sleep
leaving their troubles all over the house
like the child's toys,
and taking a few with them too.

On the back porch a gray cat
turns her face into the moonlight and watches the snow fall.
This house, without its television
its queer troubled voices leaning over the table
is like the inside of a closed music box.
And the big people?
They're drifting off, getting smaller.

The Arranged Hours

Sleepless, I get up
trudge about the house
and then remember ...

my friend, seven years old, getting out of bed
on Far North winter nights
to stand at the cabin window
and look out across a snowlit clearing

where the flickering eyes of timber wolves edged closer.
So that by daylight he fell asleep with his secret
and dreamwalked through the day,
an illness no one could diagnose.

And now all I can do is stand at this window
staring at the lights of the city until
my legs wobble and I fall back out
of the arranged hours the desk and chair of boredom
the seasons divided and recorded these the countries I live in

and some dream of my own, or poem, or flurry of wings
rises from the black water of night
and passes over the far trees.

And even then a part of it returns
like a fever
circling the dark restful hours
waiting for me at daylight
keeping its distance.

From a Photograph

In your checkered dress you are smiling
your blond hair diffused in the angelic light of a poor
  exposure.
You are seven or eight,
wearing white anklets and shoes with buckles
standing with your hands behind your back.
But where is the farm on Territorial Road
and the fruit orchards of Coloma?
Where is the black bread and blood sausage
and where is Latvia, that dark stain on Russia's shoulder?
All I can see is a hedgerow behind you,
marigolds and chrysanthemums gone wild
in the saffron light of October.
But of course I know where they are—the trains of 1944
are still lugging their cargo westward and your father
is still on that bicycle in Poland trying to catch up.
So why do I wonder how we will manage across the years
and how we will find each other?
I look again. You are still standing there
happy, or maybe just smiling for the camera.
Someone released the shutter
and somehow missed almost everything.

Seashells, Cape Hatteras

—To Kristine

Here is cinnamon streaked with tartar
the mollusk's fan of clove and pearly onion
a cockleshell black as pepper
and one of salt with two waves of plum breaking across its
    ridges.
The scallop has rubbed up against a peach
and the whelk has fallen down a spiral staircase of breakers.

Returning from my long walk down the beach
where the brooding waves swept the sand
from beneath my feet at every step
I still refuse to walk on higher ground.
You turn to me and smile,
your toes curled into the sand, ten translucent shells
of your own among the chipped and shattered ones.

White mustard, tarragon, blanched almond
like lessons you must learn by rote
you sift them carefully, your head bowed in play.

Late December, No Sign of Snow

The days were so brief then
the last insects barely had time to die.
Broomfuls of long grass the color of almonds
swept across the field in waves that broke with the wind.
The hunchback foothills with their scrub oaks
looked like a pencil sketch or
like one of those first photographs
brought back from the moon.

And the man inside that house
perched on a hill between seasons
was weightless. No weather in the heart.
A bellyful of inertia.
He was waiting for his life to get right.
Where was the wife?
She was working, piling on the guilt.
You know the story—
another day another dollar.
Someone had to do it.

The Other One

Ten below zero
moonlight
and the ice-bird roosting under the eaves again
shedding tiny feathers on the windowpane
that stick like fingerprints.

The winter night clinks shut around the house.

It is only January but I have been watching
the days grow longer and the light of supper
edge up into the clouds above
the bleary-eyed men lined up along the horizon.
Even at this hour I can still see the one that won't go home.

The snow keeps falling down my father's face.

On the kitchen table is my son's uneaten dinner,
something else left unfinished
but I won't start on that one now.
It is time to enter dark rooms
and steal what I can of lives that are finally peaceful.

I am fading inside like my image in the window.

I bend over my wife, only her forehead showing
beneath quilts and pillows.
In the other room the small one is sprawled like a cat,
and later when he cries out
I will go in and we will pretend together:

The bad things have to go away when we tell them to.

But now what about the other one in the room upstairs?
He has little left to steal and guards it well
so what's the point?

He is waiting faithfully, staring
out at the snow swirling around the streetlamp.
He wants his life back.
And he wants his cookies and milk.

For Inese

Across two thousand miles
of crossed telephone wires your voice
barely broke clear
over the roar of the ocean
the clicks and hisses
the long windy voices of night rising
from the fields stretched between us
I listened
heard you say you were recovering
heard a man on another line
say he was tired too
as if, for a moment, he was speaking to us
and heard the static rise and cover us all.

Crow, Grandfather

The crow again
the black as night again
the human voice scratched out along the curve of a wing,
perpetual scowl flying off through the trees . . .

grandfather, some older version of loneliness
glinting in your crow eyes
is that you?

Down the street a bulldozer is grinding away
making a big hole in the earth bigger.
More of something here, less somewhere else.
Someone's life.

Might as well take it all—
the gummy chunks of clay
the stones that little boys throw
the rocks that the massive shining blade strikes with a thud,
all the stuff we call something

nothing like air, light, a thought streaking forward into the
    eyes.
Nothing like living.

In the sky to the north
a black bird with an iron weight in his heart lumbers off.

The crow again
the black as night again
old man who told me life was hard
and meant to be.

III

Why care if birth and death are merely points
when life is not a straight line?
Why torment yourself eyeing the calendar
wondering what is at stake?

—Vladimir Holan,
tr. by Jarmila and Ian Milner

Inside a Life

Too tired to move, I sit amongst a heap of toys
wife and child asleep
the long day put to bed
the long thoughts just beginning
and who needs them?

In my hand is a blue box that goes inside
a red box that goes inside a green one,
and I can't help think that inside my life
is my father's and inside his
one that is too small—missing the cornfields
my grandfather sold off when he lived too long
and ran out of money.
Imagine—living too long.

As the hour gets later my life gets out of hand.

Tomorrow it's my turn to get up,
to see my son's face before anything else and
remember daylight entering a field.
And already I am inside his life as he takes
his first words from my lips and gives them back,
his one year burning like a big stone of granite
with its million knife-points sparkling in the afternoon sun.
All that knowledge.
Who wouldn't like to sit down and rest
and maybe never get up again?

In the supermarket this morning
I saw the girl I loved in high school,
the face I still see inside my dreams
and I turned away
for there too was the darkness pushing
its blinding freight of light ahead of it,
star-years away but the news moving closer.

It's too much for one evening, for one man
in the middle of the beginning of a child's life.
Inside the past that is inside the present inside the future.
I pick up a puzzle with only four pieces—
rabbit, cat, big dog, and little dog.
This should be easy.

Walking at Midnight

We follow the deer trails
hundreds of cleft hearts
chiseled into ice-crusted snow—
one day's coming and going on top of another
like our own lives
until it is the clearest path to take
the easiest

That must be why we are walking
in this Wisconsin woods at midnight,
in the house far behind us—our wives talking softly
and your two girls asleep in their snowlit room.

Now, out into some farmer's newly cleared field
we step carefully among big stones with masks of snow
and clumps of frozen earth that shine like black porcelain.

From out of the half-buried weedstalks
a fieldmouse hops victoriously before us.
We bend down to inspect his faint brushstrokes
as if looking for clues.
Our knees creak like chilled glass.

For a moment I imagine that beyond this empty plane of
    snow
the future centuries are waiting like enormous dark towers,
a few lights on in the upper windows
where some judgments are being made.

Trying to Write

At the typewriter he is trying to write
but in the rapidfire of the keys he hears an execution.
The condemned man is standing against a white stone wall
in the blank light of dawn.
Each volley of black letters pierces his heart
but he stands up, brushes off his coat
and still he won't confess the sins against his family.
So the son fires again—
words pass through his father's heart like cold air
until it is a sieve
and the morning light of the whole midwest shines through it
and the tears of his wife catch in it and glisten
and his daughter's nervous laughter
tickles him painfully as it falls through.
In the dirt of the courtyard
a few big splashes print the letter *o,*
a small sigh
or maybe it's nothing.

A Terrible Life

He comes home without any money.
She says nothing.
And so it goes in the big crazy house by the woods
white with black shutters, the number on the mailbox
but no one visits.
It rains all spring into eleven pans in the kitchen.
Life is terrible, she says.
The last light of day crawls to the edge of the woods,
lies down beneath leafless trees
and dies belly up.
Night drops its heavy playthings into their sleep.
But whatever they are dreaming,
of clay bells from their wedding
first wildflowers
sparrows fluttering in the unmowed grass,
it is the sound the cat's tongue is making
as she laps up rainwater from one of eleven pans
set out to catch whatever in a terrible life.

Crooked Lake, 1978

It is October and the air
is like cellophane about to break.
I lean against a cold windowpane the way
I lean against the weeks and months and do nothing
but remember the summer on the lake when I closed my
    eyes
and hung from an inner tube in the deep water like an
    uprooted weed,
and also the dark days when a leaden rain
banged on the cabin roof until the cat was frightened out of
    her wits.

And some evenings when the lake was steely and seamless
the houses across the water backing up into the woods,
a few voices jangling . . .
the cat and I sat in the unmowed grass
watching fireflies that lit up like her eyes
her worries long gone
others coming on like the lights on the opposite shore.
Soft.   Distant.   Taking their places.

A Small Joy or Sadness

Two children left a dead rabbit
on the hill by our house.
Their mother said it would be happy there
in the sun where it could
rot quickly and feed the insects.
Their father said dead rabbits
are neither happy nor unhappy.
The children, showing great wisdom
said, "Papa, how do you know
a dead rabbit can't feel happy?
How do you know, Papa?"

Tonight, sitting at the kitchen table
I look out the window and see
a dog lying in the road.
I'm reminded that the dead rabbit
disappeared several days ago
the question unresolved.
From the setting sun a stream of light
runs the length of the table ending
in a warm spot on my chest.
The third button of my shirt holds a tiny rainbow
and everything—the dog, the beauty of the sunset,
the children—lies between what begins
in a great mystery out there, and ends
in a small joy or sadness here.

Memorial Day

There are no headstones
only ten acres of Kentucky bluegrass
and today
ten acres of greenhouse flowers at full bloom—
potted geraniums, purple carnations
a wreath of sweetheart roses.

Two blocks away
the leadbottomed sun droops over the sidewalk,
the sky caving in around it.
A jet pushes straight up through disintegrating clouds
into the blue, behind it
a vapor trail like a white tendril unfolding in slow motion.

At my back the last pigment of blue
bleeds into the treetops at the fenceline across the field.
I stand with my hands in my pockets
trying to watch it happen—
moths rise out of the grass, thousands
of gray wings, the cool ashes of dusk.

I walk in along the asphalt road
and stand by a heart-shaped isle of grass called Babyland.
From March 1969 to October 1969
from June 1974 to February 1975 . . .
the wishes of their mothers and fathers gone like a whisper.

The beloved sons and daughters are somewhere else
out of reach now
like the pilot with the sun still on his face
who would just once like to keep going.

Tonight, Sitting Down to Write

The window strays black.
I'm coming, I shout, I'm coming.
She stops.
Her hands are like ice, I refuse
their blind flutterings toward me.
Her back turned
she answers into the wind—
Okay, I'm waiting.
I look again, further away and closer.
What do I see—a few lights in the distance
their blank faces turned toward me, and
my deaf-mute reflection trapped in glass.

Afraid to Speak

I have been afraid to speak for a long time.
My own handwriting scares me
with its familiar artless curves and wandering arcs.
No one wants *this* I think
and my hand stops in the middle of a stroke and
will go no further, knowing that the word it's writing
comes to an end, a little wisp of ink flares into the blank
white sky of the page like the gray tail of a cloud,
and the emptiness that separates it from the next word
is greater even than my uncertainty
my failing trust in the world.

But spare them the personal misery, this poem
is threatening to disintegrate.
It wants to make more room in the world for my self-pity.
If the pen hand stops for more than a second
it grows comfortable in its resting place, like a rock.
It could remain perfectly still on the coolness
of the page under the shade of the drowsing head for a
    millennium.
But the forefinger and thumb keep pushing and pulling
and the little finger is down on its knees
taking the weight of each word.

Giving Birth

Now I bend over you, whoever you are
and say aloud the name we've chosen
Benjamin, son of my right hand
because someone has told me a child in the womb
can hear the voices circling the hill above.
And there are nights when peace comes to the house
and your mother lowers her head to that part of her that
   is you
and sings a song her mother sang to her
about a small boat crossing a big lake.

*

To make a frame to hold the first picture
I pry up an oak board from a packing crate,
knock the nails loose
and sand off the skin of dirt until I can run my finger
down the bare wood and taste the swampy odor of oak.
Deep in the wood it is raining.
Through the flecks in the grain I can almost see a house
and a small face at the window.

*

Inside the ear, in that tiny airless courtyard
where I still hear my mother calling me to supper
the light gives up,
unable, as we all know, to bend around corners.
Some things even light cannot do.
So it is that everything we hear passes through darkness,
the first voices hovering over us
and the last.

*

Beneath the moon swelling for the ninth time we wait.
I stand at the window watching a snowfall
that looks like it won't stop.
The empty picture frame is leaning against the workshop
  wall
beside my hammer and my father's saw.
And the small boat is still on the big lake.

Our Bodies Falling Through the Heavens

"Self-contemplation is a curse
That makes an old confusion worse."
                    —*Theodore Roethke*

1.

Winter pulls away on its bonecrushing wheels.
The salt is spilled on the table
and I bend to lick it up.
It tastes like the story I keep telling
about the sadness of beginnings
the hands holding up the head
the runner lifting his feet
the moon a curl of wood planed from an oak board
and bubbles of light beneath the pond ice
and always the pencil and paper
these instruments of distance.

2.

Rain and more rain.
Six days.
Everything darker and smaller
in a room where the air has grown roots
until finally light scatters its fibers against the window
like iron shavings on a magnet.
And I taste the fragrance of a dried orange
with a hundred cloves stuck in it.
Another season moves through me.

3.

In the cool summer mornings
starlings arrive in threes and fours
pearly-eyed and sleek
their head feathers crowned with an iridescence like wisdom.
Crossing the yard, they bow to the earth many times.
As the day thickens, a sweat bee zigzags in the sweet air
around the peach I've bitten into.
His feet, dangling like loose threads
brush the hairs on the back of my hand,
the first time anything has touched me in months.

4.

Busy hands are happy hands my grandmother said.
I can smell the damp cedar shingles
in the woodshed beside her ramshackle house
and feel the pool of silk in the rainbarrel
as I give this fragrant board
to the fierce loneliness of the power saw.
The dust drops off the workbench
into a cylinder of lamplight,
gone before I can think
of how everything becomes something else
good or bad
and how I am drifting out of myself
like one of those days in September
when we are lying on the earth like children
panes of sunlight tipping over in the wind
and our bodies falling through the heavens.

All Day

The bushes are red as lash marks,
a cold December day on fire at the edge of the marsh

and the common ones—tree sparrow
and song sparrow with strands of wheat on his chest—
make a few dry notes in the dry air,
twigs breaking.

Behind me, where the morning began—
my wife, sleeping
and my work where I left it.

Before me in the frozen mud of an old footprint
are a thousand maybe five thousand slivers
of crystalline ice that shatter soundlessly,
miles away in the forest of their microscopic world.

I would like to be that far away
and today, I almost am.

A milky pane of ice in a wheel rut squeaks underfoot.
I break open a spot with the toe of my boot
pry up a sheet the size of a tabletop
and hold it up to the sun.

*

A few more hours sink below the water.
I keep moving.
My fingers have stopped listening
to the warm brain in its safe tower of thoughts
my mouth, too numb to make a word, doesn't have to.
I understand these frost-covered wetlands
this man stiff with cold
moving through cockleburrs and buckthorn,

the chickadees and juncos in the boughs of the hemlock
the sunlight crinkling on the river water
and the big doe crashing up the embankment
to the top of the ravine where she stopped and looked back,

and beyond the cornfield where the rows deadend:
spent milkweeds, scarlet cones of staghorn sumac
a scattering of frowzy cattails.

*

All day I followed the honking of geese
until finally I saw them breaking above the trees
in gray winter twilight, and then turning away
the stitches coming loose
until they were gone and I just stood there
hands in my pockets.
Green scarf around my neck.
Looking.

Letter at the End of Winter

The creek, its dark spring waters
rushing into next week.
From where it rains
in the woods of lifeless trees
from where the water turns over
under gray skies like a snake
flashing its belly saying I am dead
can't you see I am dead.
In the culvert where the stream
crosses under the road—
bread crumbs and spastic fish.
To where the muskrat chugged upstream
with a twig in his teeth or
sat gnawing roots on the muddy bank.
The roots, hairless albino creatures
who never say a word.
The mallard drake and his brown woman.
Where did they go the next day?
Crows with their rusty bicycle horns
their worn-out pair of false wings
always too heavy for them.
A kettleful of blackbirds pours across
the sky. This is it this is it.
And the wind that can't say no.

Walking in My Grandfather's Fields

I listen to field sparrows
breaking open their kernels of song
and follow the old way down a dirt path
through thistles and goldenrod.

It is August again,
the warm hand of death is on the earth
the sky filled with pale tea
where the sun fell below the fenceline . . .

fell and kept falling
into that kingdom where bluejays
picked at the garnets of blood beneath the mulberry tree
and the nights were moonless fields hemmed with barbed
    wire.

When the day retreated
my grandfather sat on the cement steps of his house
reading the sports page by a yellow forty-watt bulb.
Watch it boy, he said, joking and serious
when I got too close.

Now, old Dutchman, ten years have grown up
between your death and my life,
your house has been razed, my own is not in order
and I'd like to know
which is it, should I laugh or cry?

For here is the milkweed making a hundred wishes
that one may come true
and there are two goldfinches
trying to erase the sky again.

About the Author

Don Stap grew up in the farm country of southwestern Michigan. He received a B.A. from Western Michigan University and a Ph.D. from the University of Utah. After several years of teaching he worked as a free-lance journalist, writing primarily about natural history subjects for such magazines as *Sierra, International Wildlife,* and *Travel & Leisure.*

His poems have appeared in many journals since 1972, and for eight years he was editor of *Westigan Review.* In 1986 he received a Creative Writing Fellowship in poetry from the National Endowment for the Arts.

A book he is writing about ornithologists studying the birds of South America, for which he has made several trips to remote areas of Peru, will be published by Alfred A. Knopf, Inc.

He now lives in Florida with his wife and son, and teaches at the University of Central Florida.